LAST NIGHT AT THE WURSTHAUS

New and Selected Poems

LAST NIGHT AT THE WURSTHAUS

New and Selected Poems

Doug Holder

GREY SPARROW PRESS, INC.
St. Paul, MN

Last Night at the Wursthaus:
New and Selected Poems

First Edition: September 1st, 2017

Author: Doug Holder
Introduction: Nina R. Alonso
Cover Designer: Steve Glines

ISBN: 978-1974606269

Principal Editor: Diane Smith
Copy Editor: Timothy Stobierski
Electronic Editor: Joseph Michael Owens
Graphic Designer: Steve Glines
Original Photograph of the Wursthaus Courtesy of the
Cambridge Historical Society, Cambridge, MA

All rights to *Last Night at the Wursthaus: New and Selected Poems* by Doug Holder are reserved with Grey Sparrow Press. No part of this publication may be reproduced or distributed in any form by any means, or stored in a database or retrieval system, without the prior written consent of Grey Sparrow Press, including, but not limited to, any network or other electronic means of transmission, or broadcast for distance learning. ©Individual copyright remains with the writer and photographer for their respective work. Grey Sparrow Press rights remain with Grey Sparrow Press, St. Paul, Minnesota 55121.

GREY SPARROW | St. Paul

For my wife Dianne Robitaille

CONTENTS

Introduction, Nina R. Alonso, i

Last Night at the Wursthaus, 2
Looking at a Lone Woman in a Bar, 3
"No Man Steps into the Same River Twice," 4
Filene's Basement-Boston, 5
Blondes, 6
Archetypes of Harvard Square, 7
Death of a Homeless Man, 8
I Am Willy Loman, 9
My Mother Prepares Me for Death, 11
The Newspaper, 13
My Father's Fedora, 14
Wild Boars at Savenor's, 15
Modern Lovers, 16
"Oh Don't," she said. "It's Cold." 17
The Bronx, 1965, 19
A Hollow Man, 20
He Wore Shoes a Size Too Small, 21
The Lottery Ticket, 22
Professor Irwin Corey, 23
First Apartment, Boston, 1978, 25
Lung Cancer: Stage 4, 27
My First Poetry Reading, 29
A Dog Digging Up His Master's Grave, 30
A Vacant Stare at the Sky, 31
Living in your Pajamas, 32
For Sidewalk Sam, 33
I Texted, 35
The Big Bang, 36
A Mother Leads Her Child to the Men's Room, 37
Mice, 38

Biography, 39
Words of Praise, 40
Acknowledgements, 41

INTRODUCTION

by Nina R. Alonso

One of Doug Holder's poems quotes Heraclitus, "No man steps in the same river twice," but his writing generates double-vision, the feeling of past as present, existing in the flow of continual change.

We're in Harvard Square's Wursthaus (now replaced by a faceless bank) overhearing the flow of vintage chatter, then watching a man scratch losing lottery tickets one after the other, then in a too quiet Harvard library where "caged scholars/circle their wired cages like rats/gnawing on manuscripts." In Filene's Basement he's shopping, as "it was a place to go when you're happy or desperately hurt."

He shifts to the Bronx where ancient Jewish women sit on lawn chairs and his Uncle Dave called George Gershwin 'a good kid.' These people and places are familiar to me and to many of us who lived in the same space and island of time, understand eyes that see through our adult guise to what we were like in junior high: "You can't/bullshit the blonde/ she knows."

The book has integrity, cuts to heart center, but without a shred of excess. There's no hype, no axe to grind, nothing being sold to us. We know his mother from our own, "At night/ the murmur of the dead/ hover around her bed." I grew up in the neighborhood he rails against when he "screamed/ my screed/ against the suburbs/ the conspiracy of broad lawns/ and narrow minds."

This world is under construction, bought and sold daily, repeatedly dug up, repaved, pieces erased, replaced and so full of invasive sales hype that we can't even remember what was there before. We need this writer who sees and remembers to keep us centered, strengthen us, help us see what's there, help us resist. Doug Holder's writing has subtlety and substance, an authenticity that sustains.

~~

Nina R. Alonso's poetry appeared in *Ploughshares, The New Yorker, The New Boston Review, Ibbetson Street, Muddy River Poetry Review, Bagel Bards, Black Poppy Review, Sumac, MomEgg,* and more. Her stories (one a Pushcart nominee) were in *Southern Women's Review, Tears and Laughter, Broadkill Review,* and recently *Peacock Literary Review.* Her book, *This Body* was published by David Godine Press. She edits *Constellations: a Journal of Poetry and Fiction,* is director of Fresh Pond Ballet School, and formerly taught at Boston Ballet. She practices Heartfulness meditation and has traveled to India many times.

Original Photograph of the Wursthaus
Courtesy of the Cambridge Historical Society
Cambridge, Massachusetts

LAST NIGHT AT THE WURSTHAUS

How I miss
that hush from the Square
the dark oasis
contemplating my beer
as things come to a head.
The ancient waitresses
their surliness an art
bark the orders
through the swing of doors.
And at the bar
scholars of the academy
and everyday scholars of life
share the same expanse of polished wood.
I used to strain
to hear the bits of wisdom
old man Cardullo spit from
his cigar-studded mouth
the rancorous jokes
the cops told
huddled around him
in an enigmatic cabal.
And now
at this same corner
pretty boys on posters
smile,
with hardened torsos
and I am swept away
to wherever...
the crowd goes.

LOOKING AT A LONE WOMAN IN A BAR

They are always so impenetrable.
A dead stare at the wall.
Her drink
some half-empty prop.
And the cigarette...
Still holding a torch
but for what?

No—
my gaze will not be met.
And she will walk out the door.
And the clues
she will leave
a certain dead end.
And the cigarette will smolder
and the smoke
will follow its trail...

"NO MAN STEPS INTO THE SAME RIVER TWICE"

—Heraclitus

Put your foot in the water again.
The river engulfs your toes
in a serpentine swirl,
you feel the hard grain
of the dirt bed
but something's amiss.
Could it be the fins
of that minuscule fish?
The ripples on the water
its scribble now
an indecipherable
text.

The clouds above are not parted
the beams of light
still in the closet.
The iconic rock
a wee-bit diminished
the stone face cracking,
yes—something is
lacking.

And the tree
and the bird
perched on it
sings a new, beguiling
sonnet…

FILENE'S BASEMENT-BOSTON

And the doors could barely contain them.
The thoroughbred ladies.
Ready to race
at the stroke of the clock's hand
for discount linen and lace.

And I was swept in
by an animated, cackling
feminine wave,
soon eyeing
the salesman
eyeing me
as I was transformed—
polished into a well-heeled
businessman
in a double-breasted suit,
and the clerk cracked by my side
"Hey, kid, ain't she a beaut?"

And I fingered the starched
collars of multi-colored
Arrow shirts
and I admired the crusty, ancient saleswoman
who still had the desire and energy to flirt.

And where else
could you drape your wounds
with a funky Fedora
or the balm of a soft,
slightly irregular Brooks Bros. shirt
it was a place to go when you were happy
or desperately hurt.

BLONDES

They always will
intimidate you.
Even in your sixth decade—
those judgmental Barbies
blonde, blue-eyed
roll their eyes
and do a clandestine text
and yet
you still try to
win them over—

Stooped
your beard
white with regret
but you don't forget
the pain
and their pert disdain
in some ancient high school hall,
the pecking order
you clad in polyester
and body odor.

Oh, but you
are older
you teach with
glasses perched
on the bridge of your nose
your class
and you
in both your
early morning pose.

But you can't
bullshit the blonde
she knows.

ARCHETYPES OF HARVARD SQUARE

The Babel
and babble of
all these tongues—
the caged scholars
in the bowels

of the Widener library
circle their
wired cages
like rats
gnawing on manuscripts—
the timeless
raven-haired girl
peasant skirt
a clasp of books
held close to her ribs.
In the pit
"The Branded"
jaded with nostril rings
flashing studded tongues
coiled serpentine tattoos.

The entitlement
of the bold titles
that scream for recognition
from bookstore windows—
the winding street—
the florid, bearded face
of the chess master
his calculating stare

Oh,
and yes...
I'm there.

DEATH OF A HOMELESS MAN

Last thing I remember
I laid on the grates
of the Boston Public Library
I was lifted up by
the waft of its
warm mist
I looked down
to a figure in a dirty parka
long nails like a raccoon
the intricate, matted mosaic
of hair.

I saw a woman
touch me with the cold,
metallic tip of her
fashionable shoe.

Oh! Cradle me
Cradle me
in your arms!
I am not a stick
or merely a bone.

I was a boy running through a meadow
my skin smelled like baby's milk
my eyes were not clouds
but brilliant suns
I laid on my back
and searched the skies
like now
before I
died.

I AM WILLY LOMAN

I hear my wife say,
"Attention must be paid...,"
as I carried my heavy bags
my round shoulders
to her face.

"They love me, they love me in Somerville,"
I said to myself,
the wind's hollow howl
the cat's wide-eyed shock
his questioning meow
as I went out
to a 5AM cold.

I had my shoes shined the other day
and pressed the threads
on my threadbare jacket
ready to plaster a smile
on my tired face
to shoot the same old shit
another round of pitches
bombast and bluster
for a few
brittle bones.

Sometimes those voices reappear—
my father
grabbing his morning vodka
from the icebox
"I think I failed you,"
he said.
Captured in dementia
and the maudlin.

It is another night
with Canadian Club

humming
under my breath
to Chet Baker's
"Let's Get Lost."

My cat
pounces on imaginary prey
and so do I.
I sip
and my night
will slip
to another
inevitable day.

MY MOTHER PREPARES ME FOR DEATH

She wants me to stay in a hotel
she hides in her home
like an old house cat
before her costume
a pasted on
public face.

At night
the murmur of the dead
hover around her bed.

She can't understand
what ails her.
Is the pain
in for a permanent
stay?

And the doctors croon,
"Take one of these dear
you will feel
better soon."

We face each other
in a dark corner
of a
plastic suburban cafe.

We know what lies in
our receding gums
the tip of our coffee-
stained lips,
the fantasy of our
flesh.

In silence
we have said it all—

more or
less.

And
at night
the murmurs
of the dead
hover around
her bed.

THE NEWSPAPER

The Long Island Railroad—
all the *Dashing Dans*[1]
fortresses of print—winged tabloids
and fedoras
the headlines
splayed on the
counter in the bar car—
"Headless Body in Topless Bar"
And the long scrolls
of newspapers
in the Boston Public Library
felt like
I was reading the Torah.
The morning coffee,
the slap of the rag
on my table,
my glasses—
four eyes are
now part of the
ritual.

At night
I saw the
New York Times
flutter in the wind
an ephemeral bird
flapping toward a street light
to come out of
the dark.

---

[1] Dashing Dan was an emblem on the Long Island railroad, phased out in 1966.

MY FATHER'S FEDORA

Surprising
after dusting it off
it was a template
for my head.
The rakish
angle
was his
in an old snapshot.
And it seemed the
right time
to crown myself
with his weathered Stetson—
an understated
red feather
waving from
an old
black band.
And for a moment
I swear
I could feel
the brush
of his
warm,
ancient, hand.

WILD BOARS AT SAVENOR'S[2]

Imagine…
what a place for wild boars.
Pressed into a tamed-tenderloin
for the most cultivated
and savage Cambridge tongue.

And forgive me—if I slip away to the "Hong Kong"
and gorge on an unapologetically greasy:
Egg Foo Young.

---

[2] Savenor's is a gourmet market in Cambridge, MA

MODERN LOVERS

At the Sherman Cafe—Somerville, MA

Lovers—
Joined at the hip,
They sit.

Across the small table
Hand on his mouse
The other on
The folds of her
Draping blouse.

He sends an amorous message
To the inbox
Of her wireless
Beating heart—

And says the very
Same things
Lovers have
Always said
From the start.

"OH DON'T," SHE SAID. "IT'S COLD."

For Rita Holder

"I'm depressed
I'm old."

I held her hand
"Oh don't," she said.
"It's cold."

She said,
"Maybe I pushed too much
Maybe I gave in much too soon,
Perhaps it was something
I needed to be told."

I held her hand,
"Oh, don't," she said.
"It's cold."

I said,
"But we love you
what was once bought
has now been long sold."

I held her hand,
"Oh don't," she said.
"It's cold."

She said:
"What should I have seen?"
What was I meant to be?
What would have pleasured me?"

I held her hand:

"Too bad" she said.

It's warm now
but oh so old."

Her hand
gently
broke from me
and like spotted moths
fluttered free.

THE BRONX, 1965

All those ancient Jewish women on lawn chairs—as I
walked by they pinched my cheeks as if I was a piece of
prime meat. "Such a nice boy, he is Minnie's grandson,"
they crowed. These old women—once their now deflated
breasts—fed their children shtetl milk. And in the hall of
my grandmother's building—a waft of Eastern European
cooking—I could Daven—like a religious man: "kishka,
herring, schmaltz, borscht, flanken, blintzes, chopped
liver…amen." My grandmother—senile— scolded my
father, "You went all over Europe, you were a playboy!" My
father replied: "Ma! I was in the army—World War II!" "A
playboy, a playboy," she muttered. Uncle Dave, a rare book
dealer, Homburg hat, cane, never cracked a smile, a brilliant
bald head under the lights—started out selling books on
pushcarts in the Lower East Side— "I had to make a
living," he explained—called George Gershwin—" A good
kid." He grew up with him—urchins darting up and down
the street, roasting spuds in back alleys—there was music—
Klezmer, jazz, the neighs of horses, the come-on from
peddlers, prayers on tenement rooftops, the cooing of
pigeons on fire escapes…

A HOLLOW MAN

For T.S. Eliot

You can
see him on the
dead-end street,
his neck craned
like a nearsighted
giraffe
his feet splayed
unsure
of what direction.

You know
the skin flakes
and drifts to
the ground
when it
is untouched
and the hands
curl like a fetus
in need of
its mother.

You can smell him
like some
moth-eaten thing
hanging limply
on the rack
held
by a tenuous thread.

And behind
his blue eyes
the fire
is long
dead.

HE WORE SHOES A SIZE TOO SMALL[3]

They always told him
"Contain yourself."
And what surged through
him stopped at his feet.
The blood
bursting through
the crooked tributaries of his toes
the contours
of each foot's
arching vein.
It splashed
against the
leathery walls,
the black shoelaces
curved like
a hunchback's spine
diving to the
darkened
recesses—
to be
smashed
by his gait
in the
soul
of the
shoe.

---

[3] I was told that this was a practice by Norman Rockwell.

THE LOTTERY TICKET

In the Harvard Square Starbucks
he pops a prescription.
The coffee has long
gone cold.
A swirl of sour milk
pocks its surface.
His tickets
have been scraped
of any value.
And the Herald
crossword
is still
a puzzle.
Every hour or so
he asks me to watch his seat
and he comes up
with another ticket,
and looks out the window
at a boutique square
his wasteland now.
He has got the itch
he scratches again
only to reveal
a dead-on-arrival number.
Another trip to the urinal
but hope springs eternal
and as he has done for years
he scratches
he scratches
at the
surface.

PROFESSOR IRWIN COREY[4]

A tangential precedent
remains an archetypal paradox
of indigenous tribes.
As explained
in the Updike trilogy
we must remember
that the Millennials
will meander
and be mired
in a state of inertia
and Iowa.
Move forward
move backward
but never look forward
or backward.
And beware of his handshake
it hides a snake
and a knuckle sandwich.
In the end
mutual friends should
invest in mutual funds.
Death holds a monopoly
and it is
no board game.

Don't be
a nattering nabob
but prove beyond
a point
that you pontificate and pray
to the Pope
in your
ex- cathedra
And remember ISIS

---

[4] The world's foremost expert

caused a crisis
and they will never
like us.
A parting note
for my barber,
who runs a clip joint
and is a generous man with cutting remarks.

FIRST APARTMENT, BOSTON, 1978

I woke up
by the lethal click
of a mousetrap
death by
the sticky seduction
of peanut butter.
The black
backs of
roaches
scurry to work
when the light
switches on.
And the cackle
of the cracked wooden floors
to the bathroom
down the hall.
I do a litmus
test with a thin
sheet of toilet paper
on the throned seat.
The phlegm cough
of the pensioner
next door,
the waft of red sauce
streams through the window
from Davio's below—
a fragrant and stale front
meet for a
weather change
in my room.

The shadowed silhouettes
of college girls
across the alley
a nightly screening—
rated R...wishing for X.

The screech
of the feral cat
the car,
a pen
a paper
my door just
slightly ajar.

LUNG CANCER: STAGE 4

For Jim Resnick

We sat together
at Panera Bread.
He smiled
the spaces
between his brown teeth
corrupted his mouth,
the long chain
of smoking
tainted his skin
to cigarette ash,
his eyes
seemed
like they were
ready to pop from their sockets
to flee
the ruin of his body
before it collapsed.

I asked him:
"If you could do it again…?"
He said:
"I wish my parents
sent me to a private school."

And I thought of that child
blushing from the sweet taunts
from playmates
the calls of an elusive girl
from a distant corner,
a playground
on a sultry
summer afternoon.

All before
the lungs
took in
that lethal breath
that smoky, numbing sting,
to quell
the snake
that swirled
and ate him
from within.

MY FIRST POETRY READING

It was when
I broke into
my father's
liquor cabinet
his celebratory
Chivas Regal
coursing through
my veins.
My tirade
on the manicured lawn
A hot Summer
Long Island evening
my neighbors
a transfixed audience
lining Revere Street
as I performed
screamed
my screed
against the suburbs
the conspiracy of broad lawns
and narrow minds
my invective breaking through
the drone of crickets
the deadening murmur
of TV sets
through open windows-
my madcap struggle
with the taciturn and very focused
police—
muscled tailors
fitting me for a straitjacket
on the lawn—
Hung over
and relishing
my performance…at dawn

A DOG DIGGING UP HIS MASTER'S GRAVE

One might think
it is just a dog
digging up a long-lost bone.
But
he is at the base of the tombstone.
Barking at the dates
of birth and death.
The paws are now blurs
this dog makes
the earth move
his nose drips
as if to water
something
that will
never
come
to life.

He wags his
dead end tail.
Trying to
Sniff out a scent,
his cheap cloying
aftershave
the cocktail hour whiskey
he liked it neat.

The dog in frustration
gnashed his
canine teeth
and falls asleep
right above
his master's
splayed
and decomposing...feet.

A VACANT STARE AT THE SKY

On the phone
my sister-in-law
her voice brittle and cracked
"Oh my God, a bomb at the marathon!"

At the radio
the Towers collapsed for me again
now—
the damning knapsack
the white smoke
lower extremities
shrapnel
the reporters constant replay
and I am fixated
worried about my own sorry ass
and then something clutched my throat
as my friends' and family's faces
a cinema of wide-eyed fear
flashed before me
wondering
if they were
at the finishing line…
was it their time?
and when was
mine?

In the aftermath
that woman's vacant stare
at the sky
as if the heavens could answer

"Why?"

LIVING IN YOUR PAJAMAS

And still
you adorn
the beat up
slippers
the fuzzy formless
pants—
with their animals,
histrionic smiles
faded to jaded smirks.

Everything remains loose
you don't let things cling
collared shirts try to define you
ties are snakes
around your thin neck.

Gerber stains
mix with Canadian Club
on your threadbare top

And it's too late to untie
you are in a knot.

FOR SIDEWALK SAM[5]

So many brushstrokes
perhaps a purple flourish
across the stolid
unforgiving asphalt.
His paint dripping
from yogurt cups.

He brushed off
the gum,
the discarded cigarette,
the tumbleweed of newspapers,
for beneath
he saw a canvas.

He needed to feel his brush
where so many pounded
the pavement.
The poseur,
the pundit,
the plaudit,
the pol,
the stumble bums,
the flash-in-the- pan.
All those men
in gray flannel suits,
the women in
their Delman heels.

The dead drunk
perhaps falling
on his art
after a sucker punch
or a child staring
down in wonderment.

---

[5] Sidewalk Sam was a famous Boston street artist.

The mayoral smile of Kevin White
a reproduction of a European master,
perhaps someone will stop to look
as our world spins faster and faster.

I TEXTED

I texted through the Tsunami
And missed a head bobbing
Like a hirsute lure signaling a fish's ravenous bite
My hands hit the keys
A midst a drowning
Man's pleas.

I texted as we made love
My fingers made sensuous curls
And lovingly touched the keys.
I never heard her murmurs:
"Please, Please."

I texted through the funeral
And did an Instagram
Of her death mask face.
I am never here
Or there
Or just
One place.

I search for some expression
On the poker face of my phone
I close the door slowly
We want to be alone.

THE BIG BANG

It's not the bang
so much
as the anticipation
the sensitive hairs
in each of your
expectant drums
your body
retreating into
its seminal
fetal curl
the hands'
feral clawing
and it all
boils
down to
some histrionic
exploding sun,
and then
quite simply
you're done.

A MOTHER LEADS HER CHILD TO THE MEN'S ROOM

And he takes her hand.
And walks into that room,
with all his reluctance,
and all its strange allure.
And it will be a woman who he will trust.
Who will teach
him the right way,
as he drops his pants
and releases a fine
and diffuse spray.

MICE

They were connected to our youth.
Those first
holes-in-the-wall.
They crashed our apartments
like they were
raucous neighborhood parties.
The snap in the dead of night
of the trap's metal, ravenous jaw—
Death?
or a glorious heist?
Of mice and men,
it was all
a game of chance—
we slipped in treacherous holes
as easily
as we slipped out—
ready for any
destination.

BIOGRAPHY

Doug Holder holds an MLA in English Literature and Language from Harvard University. He is the arts/editor for The Somerville Times, publisher of the Ibbetson Street Press, curator of the Newton Free Library Poetry Series in Newton, MA, book review editor for the Wilderness House Literary Review, and founder of the literary blog, Boston Area Small Press and Poetry Scene. He teaches creative writing at Bunker Hill Community College in Boston and Endicott College in Beverly, MA. Holder's work has been widely published by small presses with a number of collections to his credit. Holder has interviewed hundreds of poets and writers for his Somerville Media Center Show, "Poet to Poet, Writer to Writer" many of which are archived at university libraries. He recently won the Allen Ginsberg Award from the Newton Writing and Publishing Center and received a citation from the Massachusetts House of Representatives for his work as a publisher, poet, editor, and professor. He resides in Somerville, MA.

WORDS OF PRAISE

Threadbare and fedora-dashing, Doug Holder
maneuvers through cityscapes of judgmental
blondes, beheaded voyeurs, and dead men needing
affection. Along the way Holder studies the
solemn detritus that people inevitably shed, like
losing lottery tickets. No poet I know sells a retail
vision of hardened urban denizens this directly.
Artistically, the man's a closer.

—Dennis Daly, Author of *Sentinel*

No one delivers the sharp, sweet bite of nostalgia
like Doug Holder. In reading this sleek collection
you will find yourself transported back to the days
when everything was fascinating and each person
you saw had a story from the ancient, surly
waitresses barking out orders, to the blondes who
always had the power to intimidate you. Nothing
escapes the poetic eye of Doug Holder then or
now. With each new book I find myself thinking,
This is his best yet. He never disappoints. Never.

—Robin Stratton, Editor,
Boston Literary Magazine

The landscape has changed but the memories
haven't. Take a walk with these poems that bring
back the old Harvard Square, Boston, and the
Bronx. In one poem Doug writes, "I used to strain
to bear wits of wisdom." There is no strain here.
Step back into time with the characters Doug
Holder describes all contemplating their dead ends
and new beginnings.

—Gloria Mindock, Editor,
Červená Barva Press

ACKNOWLEDGEMENTS

Some of these poems have appeared in *Grey Sparrow, Boston Literary Magazine, Voices Israel Anthology, Blue Fifth Review, Cervena Barva Press, Compassionate Anthology, Everyday Writer, spoKe, Like Meanie, Turtle Island Quarterly, Stylistic Stanzas, The Boston Globe, Alternative Current Press*, and others.

Made in the USA
Middletown, DE
04 September 2017